W9-BYN-735

A Basic Mencius

The Wisdom and Advice of
China's Second Sage

Compiled by Kuijie Zhou

LONG RIVER PRESS

Compilation Copyright © 2006 Kuijie Zhou
Copyright © 2006 Long River Press
All rights reserved. No part of this book may be reproduced without written
permission of the publisher

Published in the United States of America by
Long River Press
360 Swift Ave., Suite 48
South San Francisco, CA 94080
www.longriverpress.com

Editors: Sun Lei, Philiana Ng
Cover design: Tommy Liu

Library of Congress Cataloging-in-Publication Data

Zhou, Kuijie.
  A basic Mencius : wisdom and advice of China's second sage / Compiled by
Kuijie Zhou.
     p. cm.
  ISBN 1-59265-046-5 (hardcover)
 1. Mencius. 2. Philosophy, Chinese—To 221 B.C. 3. Philosophy, Confucian.
I. Title.
B128.M324Z46 2005
181'.112—dc22

                              2005017035

First Edition, 2006

ISBN-10: 1-59265-046-5
ISBN-13: 978-1-59265-046-0
Printed in China
10 9 8 7 6 5 4 3 2 1

Contents

Introduction

The Chinese philosopher known as Mencius (a transliteration of the Chinese term *"Mengzi"*, or, simply, "Master Meng"), though perhaps not as well-known as his predecessor Confucius in the universe of Chinese philosophers, carries impressive weight in his own right as perhaps *the* major exponent of Confucian thought in the centuries after Confucius's death.

Like Confucius, Mencius emphasized the importance of humanity in the maintaining of relationships, but placed greater emphasis on the role of duty and righteousness on the part of the ruler. Indeed it was by analyzing these characteristics that if the ruler neglected his duties to the people, the latter were perfectly justified in overthrowing him. In the political milieu of the day, where many of the larger states had conquered or taken over their smaller, weaker neighbors, the idea that individual rulers would sit and reflect on Mencius's sage musings while tenuously holding onto power as their kingdoms crumbled around them must have seemed like folly.

Mencius, also sometimes known as Meng Ke, was born in 372 B.C.—more than a century after the death of Confucius—in the village of Fu in the state of Zou (located in what would today be Zoucheng City in Shandong Province). The state of Zou bordered the state of Lu, the home region of Confucius, and Mencius always said that he lived "near the home of the sage."

Like Confucius, Mencius also undertook private teaching for two decades before receiving an official post, though he eventually grew tired with officialdom and resorted to wandering about from state to state much as Confucius had done. He loved teaching, and often said one of the greatest joys in the world one is to find the most promising students and teach them. Mencius had many students. At times he would receive hundreds of disciples, all listening in rapt attention as he spoke.

His collection of essays, known simply as *Mencius*, is so important to the study of Confucian thought that it is held in high honor as the last of the so-called "Four Books" of Confucianism.

Mencius takes a different style from the previous Confucian classic *The Analects*. It is a collection of essays rather than quotations. The writings are both poignant and humorous, and abound with allegory. Many of his essays, such as "Helping shoots grow by pulling them upward" and "The deserter who retreated 50 steps mocks the one that retreated 100 steps," are still well-known even today. *Mencius* was widely quoted in the essays of the Han Dynasty (206B.C - 220A.D), and had a profound influence on writers of the Tang (618-907) and Song (960-1279) dynasties, including Han Yu, Ouyang Xiu, Zeng Gong, Wang Anshi, and Su Dongpo. In the Qing Dynasty (1644-1911) *Mencius* was included as an example of ancient writing in the *Collection of Articles from One Hundred Literary and Historical Books*, one of the greatest compilations of the era.

Mencius lived during the Warring States Period (475-221B.C), when seven bigger states: Qi, Chu, Yan, Han, Zhao, Wei, and Qin "fought over lands, killing people all over the fields; and fought over cities, filling them with dead bodies." The wars brought great suffering to the people. Mencius lamented that "the ruler has more than enough meat in his kitchen and fat horses in his stable; while the people look hungry, and corpses of the starved scatter around the field." Mencius was strongly against war, and tried to persuade the kings to adopt "rules of benevolence." He argued that "the way to win the world is to win the support and confidence of the people; the way to win the support and confidence of the people is to do what benefits them and undo what they detest." He also believed that "to a state the people are the most important, the altars to the gods of earth and grain come second, and the ruler is of the least importance." These were rare democratic and humane opinions in that era of Chinese history.

The rule of benevolence is based on the theory that all humans are born kind. Mencius thought that human nature is essentially good, the qualities of mercy are universally shared, and that everyone can become as wise as Yao and Shun, the great sage kings of old. On ethics he urged people to nurture their noble spirit.

Mencius carried on the Confucian theory of historical inevitability; that the course of history is in constant circulation, in which a great ruler appears every 500 years, and wise people rise to assist him. He also endorsed the ideas established by Confucius that there were different social classes that, while distinct, required the other to survive harmoniously, so those who work with their brains are gentlemen, and those who perform manual labor are working people. Mencius claimed that "without gentlemen, no one will rule the working people; without working people, no one will support the gentlemen." Although Mencius once staid that "it is a common rule in the world that those working with their brains rule, and those working with their brawn are ruled," he also stated that "the people are more important than the ruler."

Mencius won little applause for his ideas during his lifetime, for they were thought inane and unpractical. During the decades between his death in 289 B.C. to the unification of China by the state of Qin in 221 B.C., the warring chaos across China exacerbated to unprecedented heights, leaving no place for Mencius' seemingly arcane thoughts. After the Qin Dynasty was founded, Emperor Qin Shihuang launched a national campaign of burning Confucian books and burying Confucian scholars alive, erasing Confucianism from popular memory, and thus devastating Confucianism as a whole. The name of Mencius was also consigned into nothingness.

It wasn't until the Han Dynasty (206B.C—220A.D) that

the importance of Mencius grew again. People often mentioned the name of Zhou Gong (a renowned politician in the early Western Zhou Dynasty) in the same breath as Confucius. They called Confucius the "Supreme Sage" and his disciple Yan Yuan the "Secondary Sage."

The writings of Mencius started to gain importance in the Song Dynasty (960-1279). *Mencius* was listed together with the three classic Confucian texts, *The Analects*, *The Great Learning*, and *The Doctrine of the Mean*, as compulsory reading for the imperial examinations.

Today Mencius is known simply as the "Second Sage," coming after Confucius in importance to the world of Chinese philosophy and society. It is impossible to consider the writings of Confucius without emphasizing the role of Mencius in promoting the ongoing development of Confucian thought. Similarly, the profound impact of Confucian thought is equally important when assessing the writings and teachings of Mencius, who remains unquestionably one of China's greatest and most significant philosophers.

CHAPTER I

Will and Study

Cultivating the great moral force.

Mencius' disciple Gongsun Chou was known for his skills in the martial arts. During a talk about courage, he asked Mencius, "What are you good at, master?" Mencius replied, "I am good at cultivating the great moral force." Gongsun Chou asked, "What is that?" Mencius replied, "It is a force both wide and strong. If it is cultivated with justice and not harmed in any way, it will fill the whole universe. If morality and justice are gone, it will fade away."

A king should take the people's delight as his own delight, and take the people's sorrow as his own sorrow.

During the Western Han Dynasty, General Huo Qubing (140-117B.C) won remarkable merits in the war against the Hun invaders to the north. To reward him, Emperor Wu built him a regal mansion, and invited him to its grand opening. Huo Qubing, however, rejected such a splendid mansion, and said, "How can I think of my own home when the invaders of the nation have not been annihilated?" Huo has forever been held in high esteem for his patriotism and selflessness by subsequent generations.

A true man should not be corrupted by wealth or power, give up his principles in the face of poverty, or yield in the face of force.

Chun Jing admired warriors. He asked Mencius, "Are Gongsun Yan and Zhang Yi true men?" Mencius replied, "No, how could such people be called true men?" Chun Jing retorted, "When they get angry, even the kings fidget; when they calm down, the whole world is at peace. How can they not be called true men?" Mencius explained, "To my understanding, a true man is one of justice and kindness. When he is in power, he should follow the right course together with the people rather than intimidate them; when he is out of power, he should stick to his principles. Wealth and power cannot corrupt him, poverty cannot sway his will, and force cannot subdue him. Only such a person can be called a true man."

富貴不能淫
貧賤不能屈
威武不能移

Life is what I want. Righteousness is also what I want. If I cannot have both, I prefer righteousness to life.

One day Mencius and his disciples talked about how to make choices. Mencius thought that one should always choose the good and right path. When asked to decide between two good and right things, one has to do careful evaluation before making the decision. Mencius said, "Life is what I want. Righteousness is also what I want. If I cannot have both, I prefer righteousness to life."

When Heaven intends to bestow a great mission on a person, it will make him suffer both in mind and body, and plunge him into poverty and starvation.

During the Spring and Autumn Period (770-476 B.C) prince Chong'er of Jin was in exile for 19 years before he ascended the throne. During these years he experienced great hardship. During his days in the state of Wei he once begged for food from a farmer, but was given only a clod of dirt. The prince was furious. One of his servants soothed him, "This is a good sign, that Heaven promises you land. You should take the clod with a bow." After Chong'er became king, he dedicated all his efforts to his state, and eventually made it rich and prosperous.

Heaven gives birth to all people, and it is Heaven's will to have those who are quick in understanding to instruct those who are slow in understanding.

Mencius' disciple Wan Zhang asked, "It's said that Yi Yin got a high post from Emperor Tang of the Shang Dynasty because he asked for it. Is this true?" Mencius said, "No. Yi Yin farmed in the wasteland in Youxin. His reputation of wisdom reached Emperor Tang. So the emperor sent for him and offered him gifts. But Yi Yin rejected calmly, 'Why should I accept the offer of the emperor? How can I be more joyful than retreating to the mountains and wilderness to learn the doctrines of Yao and Shun?' After the emperor invited him three times, he changed his mind, 'Rather than living in the mountains and wilderness to study the doctrines of Yao and Shun, why should I not help the emperor become a ruler like Yao and Shun, make the people as happy as their ancestors in the age of Yao and Shun, and ensure the doctrines of the two sages being carried out? Heaven gives birth to people. It's Heaven's will to have those quick in understanding to instruct those who are not as quick. I am among those who are first enlightened, so I am obliged to help the others. If I don't take the job, who will?'"

Gaining virtue by learning from others.

Yu learnt from others how to farm, fish, and make pottery. While learning from other people, he influenced them with his noble character. When he ploughed in Lishan, all local people offered their best land to each other. When he fished in Leize, all local people offered their best fishing spots to each other. When he made pottery in Hebin, all local people produced fine and durable earthenware and offered them to each other.

Influencing the state single-handedly.

Dai Busheng, an official, suggested to the king of Song to have Han Juzhou live in his palace. Mencius asked Dai, "Do you wish that your king follow what is right? Let me tell you, if a master of the state of Chu wanted his son to learn the dialect of the state of Qi, should he hire a Qi teacher or a Chu teacher to complete the task?" "A Qi teacher of course." Dai replied without hesitation. Mencius replied. "Alright, if a Qi teacher gives the class, but the boy is surrounded by many Chu people who speak Chu dialect all the time, it is impossible for the boy to learn Qi dialect even if he is forced to try everyday. You said Han Juzhou is a good man, and therefore think he will influence the king if he lives in the palace. If everyone in the palace is as good as Han, with whom will the king commit wrong? If no one in the palace is as good as Han, with whom will the king do good? How could Han Juzhou change the king by himself?"

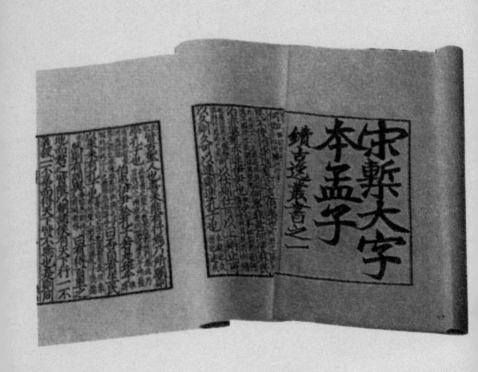

CHAPTER II

Duty and Moral Character

Everyone can become a sage.

Cao Jiao once asked Mencius, "Is it true that anyone can become a sage like Yao and Shun?" Mencius answered, "Yes." Cao said, "I heard that Emperor Wen was 10 chi tall, and Emperor Tang was 9 chi tall. I am 9.4 chi now. But I can do nothing but eat. How can I be like Yao and Shun?" Mencius was amused, "What has it to do with the height of a man? It depends on his deeds. The way of Yao and Shun is no more than being filial to parents and respectful to elders. You can become a person as great as Yao if you wear Yao's clothes, say what he would say and do what he would do." Cao Jiao expressed his wish to stay with Mencius and learn from him. Mencius said, "The way of Yao and Shun is like a broad road in front of you. Is it not that difficult to find; it is just that people don't all go that way."

Zilu was glad to have his errors pointed out.

Emperor Li Shimin (599-649) of the Tang Dynasty was a great ruler known for his readiness to hear advice from his officials. His prime minister, Wei Zheng, was forthright and candid. He had given the emperor many suggestions and criticisms, and didn't spare the emperor's feelings sometimes. But Li Shimin considered his advice carefully, and thought highly of him.

Learning from others to overcome one's own shortcomings.

In 322 B.C., Duke Ping of Lu became the king, and appointed Yuezheng Zi to handle state affairs. Mencius said, "On this news I was too happy to sleep last night." His disciple Gongsun Chou asked, "Is he tough?" "No." Mencius replied. "Is he bright?" "No." "Is he well-traveled with wide experience?" "No." Gongsun Chou was puzzled, "Then why are you happy?" Mencius explained, "I know he is ready to hear good advice from others." "Is that all?" "Yes," replied Mencius. "With this merit, he is capable to run the whole world, not to mention the state of Lu. If a person is ready to hear good advice from others, people will come to him from all areas to give their advice. If he is not ready to hear good advice, people will tell him only trifles, and he will be shunned by those who want to give him advice. If he is surrounded by flatterers all the time, how could he run the country properly?"

If one realizes his behavior is wrong, he should correct it as soon as possible.

During his stay in the state of Song, Mencius advocated reducing the farmers' taxes by carrying out tithes. Minister Dai Yingzhi argued it was better to lessen the tax this year and postpone tithes to next year. Mencius retorted, "It is like a man who steals a chicken from his neighbor every day. When he is told it is wrong to steal, he says, 'all right, I will steal a chicken every month, and will stop doing it next year.' If one realizes that his behavior is wrong, he should correct it as soon as possible. Why wait until next year?"

One should reflect on oneself whenever one fails to get the expected results. If a ruler behaves properly, all the people will pledge allegiance to him.

Mencius told his disciples, "If one loves, but cannot receive love in return, one should reflect upon whether one is benevolent. If one fails to administer others, one should reflect upon whether one is wise. If one treats others with courtesy, but gets no response from them, one should reflect upon whether one is sincere. One should reflect on oneself whenever one fails to get the expected results. If a ruler behaves properly, all the people will pay allegiance to him. *The Book of Songs* says, 'The Zhou reign was long because it conformed to Heaven's will. Be strict with oneself and blessings will descend.'"

S ay that an archer suddenly adjusts his posture before shooting. If he misses the target, he will not blame the winners, but look for the reason in himself.

When talking of benevolence, justice, courtesy and wisdom, Mencius said, "Benevolence is the noblest quality in the universe, and is the final settling place of humanity. It is not wise not to be benevolent when no one prevents you being so. If a man is neither benevolent nor wise, nor courteous, nor just, he can become nobody but a slave. If he is ashamed of being a slave when he can only be a slave, it is like a bow-maker feeling ashamed of making bows or arrow-makers feel ashamed of making arrows. If he is really ashamed, he should practice benevolence conscientiously. A benevolent man is like an archer in a match. The archer suddenly adjusts his posture before shooting. If he misses his target, he will not blame the winners, but look for the reason in himself."

The basis of the empire are its states, the basis of a state are its families, and the basis of a family are its individuals.

According to Confucian classic *The Book of Rites*, "one should cultivate his moral character before his family is in order; all families are in order before a state is under good rule; all states are under good rule before the empire is at peace." In this remark the "empire" refers to China, and the "states" are its vassal kingdoms. Mencius instructed his disciples, "There is a popular saying, 'Empire, States, and Families.' The basis of an empire are its states, the basis of a state are its families, and the basis of a family are its individuals."

修身齊家治國平天下

When Heaven sends down calamities, there is hope of surviving them; when man commits sin and consequently brings calamities upon himself, there is no way to escape.

When talking about rule of benevolence, Mencius said, "The implementation of the rule of benevolence leads to glory, otherwise, humiliation occurs. The contemporary rulers loathe humiliation, but won't carry out the rule of benevolence. It is like a person hating dankness, but living in the lowlands. If they really don't want to be humiliated, they should stress morality and respect scholars, appoint virtuous people as officials, and assign capable people to important posts. When a country is free of domestic troubles and foreign invasions, and its government is honest and enlightened, it will be feared by its neighbors that are big and strong. *The Book of Songs* reads 'repair windows and doors before a storm comes, so as to avoid losses.' The writer of this poem knew well the way to run a state. If a state is ruled in this way, who would dare offend it? Now we have no domestic troubles or foreign invasion, so those in power indulge in luxury and pleasure, ignoring government affairs. This is tantamount to seeking calamity. All one's fortunes and misfortunes are asked for by oneself. *The Book of Songs* also says, 'The Zhou Dynasty should accomplish the Mandate of Heaven and seek more fortunes.' *The Book of History* says, 'When Heaven sends down calamities, there is hope of surviving them; when man commits sin and consequently brings calamities upon himself, there is no way to escape.'"

A person will be insulted only after he behaves without self esteem; a family will be destroyed only after it collapses from inside; and a kingdom will be invaded only if it provides a cause.

Mencius told his disciples, "How can one be a colleague of non-benevolent people? Those who are nonchalant of, or even take pleasure in the misfortune of others? What they aspire after is the enjoyment that will incur disaster to states and families. If such people can become colleagues, how could disasters happen to kingdoms and families? A children's song says, 'I wash my hat in clean water and wash my feet in dirty water.' This is determined by the quality of water. So a person will be insulted only after he behaves without self esteem; a family will be destroyed only after it collapses from inside; and a kingdom will be invaded only after it provides a cause. According to *The Book of History*, one can escape from natural disasters, but one cannot escape punishment for one's own misconduct."

CHAPTER III

Handling One's Affairs

The one who does things against established rules and rites is like the one who pulls the seedlings out to help them grow.

When discussing with Gongsun Chou on how to cultivate the "great moral force," Mencius said, "We should take pains to cultivate the great moral force, but can never do it in unjustified haste." He then gave an example, "A farmer in the state of Song thought his seedlings grew too slowly, so he pulled them up higher and higher out of the dirt one by one. After a day's toiling, he went home and told his family, 'I am really tired, but I helped the seedlings grow taller!' His son hurried to the field, only to find all the seedlings had withered." Mencius commented, "There are many people in the world who would pull the seedlings to help them grow. The one who gives up cultivating the moral force when no instant effect can be seen is like one who farms but would not tend to the weeds. The one who acts against the rules is like the one who pulls the seedlings out to help them grow. Such actions do more harm than good."

Though playing the game of Go is but a pastime, it requires great skill. If one cannot devote his heart to it, he will not be able to master it.

Yi Qiu, a master of the game of Go, gave lessons to two students. One student was fully attentive in class, while the other was absent-minded. The latter student, for certain, could not make the same progress as the former, though they were in the same class. Is it because he is less intelligent than his classmate? No, but because of his absent-mindedness, he will never excel at the game and it will be but a trifle pursuit.

Acts must conform to reality.

Mencius said, "Yu preferred truth to good wine. Tang persisted in studying *The Doctrine of the Mean*, and appointed people of virtue regardless of their social status. Emperor Wen treated his people in the way of giving solace to the wounded, and never ceased to pursue the truth. Emperor Wu respected his officials in the court. Duke Zhou aspired to learn from the rulers of the Xia, Shang, and Zhou dynasties so as to carry on the achievements of Yu, Tang, Wen, and Wu. If none of his acts conformed to reality, he would sit up day and night pondering over the matter. Once he had the solution, he would sit up until dawn to put it into practice immediately."

A gentleman educates others in the way of teaching them archery. He draws the bow to the fullest, but doesn't discharge the arrow, needing only to show his eagerness to shoot.

Gongsun Chou complained, "The ideal principles are lofty and fine, but it is so difficult to attain, like climbing to heaven. Why not make them easier to reach so as to encourage people to try everyday?" Mencius said, "A good craftsman will not change his rules just to make things easier for clumsy workers. Yi would not lower his standards for archery for the sake of poor archers. A gentleman educates others in the way of teaching them archery. He draws the bow to the fullest, but doesn't discharge the arrow, needing only to show his eagerness to shoot."

T each each other's children to avoid conflict.

Gongsun Chou asked Mencius, "Generally, a gentleman does not teach his own son. Why is this so?" Mencius replied, "Because it doesn't work. Teaching must be conducted the right way. When such a way doesn't work, the teacher will get angry, and therefore hurt the student. The son will object, 'You are teaching me the good principles and right ways, but your behavior does not conform to what you told me.' This way father and son will run afoul of each other. This is not good. This is why in ancient times gentlemen taught each other's sons so as to avoid conflict between father and son."

Yin had a mirror from the Xia Dynasty, from which he could see a warning.

Mencius told his disciples, "The compass and T-square set the criteria for drawing circles and squares. Sages offer the criterion for human behavior. The kings and subjects should perform their duties respectively, and take Yao and Shun as examples. The subjects do not respect their kings if they fail to serve the latter in the way Shun served Yao. The kings do harm to their people if they cannot rule the people in the way Yao did. According to Confucius, there are only two ways to run a state, practicing the rule of benevolence, or not. A king who does harm to his people will end up ruining himself and the state as well, or at least put himself in danger and weaken the state. Emperors You and Li of the Zhou Dynasty were dishonored by their posthumous titles "You" and "Li," which can never be changed. *The Book of Songs* says, "Yin had a mirror dating from the Xia Dynasty, from which he was able to see a warning." In ancient times, an emperor, nobleman, or minister, was often given a title after his death in light of his deeds during his lifetime. The title of

"You" was given to the deceased who was deemed not to have followed proper conduct, while the title of "Li" was given to those who persecuted the innocent. Both Emperors You and Li of the Zhou Dynasty will thus always be remembered as despotic, tyrannical rulers.

A narrow mountain path will be broadened into a road if traveled frequently, but will be dense with weeds if not used for a long time.

Mencius stressed cultivation of moral character, and believed that this task required constant effort. He once told Gao Zi, another philosopher of the same age, "A narrow mountain path will be broadened into a road if traveled frequently, but will be dense with weeds if not used for a long time."

Even a plant that grows readily will die if it is exposed to the burning sun for one day and then to the bitter cold for ten days.

In the state of Qi, some blamed Mencius for not helping the king, who was foolish. Mencius retorted, "Even a
plant that grows readily will die if it is exposed to the burning sun for one day and then to the bitter cold for ten
days. I don't see the king often. Whenever I left him, those
who assist him to do evil came immediately. What can I
do with his desire to do good which had just been
bludgeoned? How can I help him become wise in such
conditions?

CHAPTER IV

In Society

V alue virtue and justice, and you will find delight in it.

Mencius once told Song Goujian, "I will tell you how I travel around to various states and give advice to the kings. I derive pleasure from it, whether I am understood or not." Song asked, "How can you derive pleasure from it?" Mencius replied, "Value virtue and justice and you will find delight in it. Scholars will not abandon the right way in adversity, nor diverge from the path of truth and justice. When they do not abandon the right way in adversity, they derive pleasure from doing so. When they do not diverge from the path of truth and justice, they do not disappoint the people. The ancient gentlemen brought benefit to all people when in power, and cultivated their own moral character when out of power. In obscurity, they would maintain their own integrity. In time of success they make perfect the whole empire."

A gentleman may have lifelong worries, but disasters will not emerge.

Mencius said, "A gentleman is different from ordinary people in that he has different ideas in his mind; for instance, he is focused on benevolence and rites. A benevolent person loves others, and a polite person respects others. Those who love others will always be loved, and those who respect others will always be respected. If a gentleman is rudely treated by another man, he will reflect on himself and say, 'I must have been unkind, or how could he treat me in this way?' If he finds he has never been unkind, but is still rudely treated, he will examine himself and say, 'I must have been insincere.' If he is sure he has never been insincere, but the other man does not change his attitude, he will say, 'this is a degenerate man. What is the difference between him and birds and animals? How can I blame a bird or an animal?' So, a gentleman has life-long worries, but no emergent disasters.

When one makes friends with others, what he should take into consideration is their virtues and nothing else.

Wan Zhang asked Mencius, "What is the principle of making friends?" Mencius replied, "The principle is not to take advantage of one's own age or rank. When one makes friends with others, what he should take into consideration is their virtues, but nothing else. Meng Xianzi was a minister who owned 100 carriages. When Meng Xianzi made friends, he didn't think of his post as minister or his 100 carriages; and his friends would not have made friends with him only if they considered his high rank.

Officials advise the king when he makes mistakes. If the king does not listen after they advise him repeatedly, the officials should resign.

King Xuan of Qi conferred with Mencius about the way to manage senior officials. Mencius asked, "What kind of senior official is Your Highness asking about?" The king was curious, "Are there different kinds of senior officials?" "Yes," replied Mencius. "Officials who are of the royal clan, and officials who are not." The king asked, "What do the senior officials of the royal clan do?" Mencius replied, "They advise the king when he makes mistakes. If he does not listen after they advise him repeatedly, they will dethrone him, and make a new king." King Xuan was taken aback at this. Mencius explained, "Don't be surprised. Since Your Highness asked me, I have no choice but to tell the truth." Regaining his composure, the king asked about the officials who were not of the royal clan. Mencius said, "They advise the king when he makes mistakes. If the king does not listen after they advise him repeatedly, they should resign."

One cannot talk with those who do harm to themselves; one cannot work with those who give up on themselves.

Mencius told his disciples, "One cannot talk with those who do harm to themselves; and one cannot work with those who give up on themselves. If one condemns benevolence and rites, he is doing violence to himself. If one thinks he cannot be benevolent or behave properly, he is despising himself, and giving up on himself. Benevolence is the shelter where one should reside; justice is the road which one should take. It is lamentable to see one refuse to reside where he should and stray from the road which he should take."

A gentleman fears his reputation will exceed his qualities.

Mencius' disciple Xu Pi asked, "Confucius often thought highly of water, did he not?" Mencius said, "Indeed, but what was it about water he admired? Water flows down from its source day and night. It fills the lowlands on the way before it pours into the sea. The quality of water that Confucius thought most highly of was its source. For the water without source is the water that may floods the pits and ditches in the rainy season, but then dries up and becomes nothing. Similarly, a gentleman is ashamed of his reputation exceeding his qualities."

Y ou will be treated in the same way as you treat others.

During a war with state of Lu, the state of Zou lost thirty-three officials, but there were no casualties among the people. Duke Mu of Zou was so annoyed at the people for not rescuing the officials who were killed that he wanted to execute them. Mencius reasoned, "In time of famine, people left home to flee from the disaster. Thousands of them starved to death in the wild, while your granaries were filled with grain and your storehouses were filled with treasures, but your officials didn't report the true situation to you. Those in power not only failed to take care of the people, but made their plight even worse. Remember that one will be treated in the same way as one treats others."

Extend your love for the elders in your family to all elders; extend your love for your children to all children.

Du Huan of the Ming Dynasty was known for his kindness. There was an old lady in his town who had nobody to depend on. When the old lady came to Du Huan for help, Du took her into his family without hesitation, though he was not rich at all. Du often told his family members to be nice to the old widow. When she was ill, he prepared her medicine, and served it to her with care. After the old lady died, he paid visits to her tomb every year.

I f the transition conforms to justice and rites, empires can change hands.

Disciple Peng Geng queried Mencius, "Isn't it excessive for you to have dozens of carriages and an entourage of hundreds of people, traveling with food and supplies from one state to another?" Mencius defended, "I will not accept even one meal if it is not right to do so; it is not improper for Shun to take over the empire from Yao if the transition conforms to justice and rites. Do you think that is excessive?" Peng Geng replied, "No. I merely think scholars should not take meals unless they work to earn them." Mencius said, "If people don't undertake different occupations, and exchange their products, the farmers will have surplus rice while some people are starving; women have surplus cloth while some people have nothing to wear. What if a person is filial to his parents at home, pays respect to elders, follows the ways of ancient sages, and teaches these virtues to scholars of the younger generation, but cannot earn his means? Do not look down upon or question people who are righteous and benevolent."

Yu was concerned about the flood victims as if he himself had allowed them to drown; Ji was concerned about the famine victims as if he himself had allowed them to starve.

Yu and Ji lived during an age of peace and justice. Yan Hui lived in the time of disorder. He dwelled in a shabby lane, and had simple food for meals. Such hardship was unbearable to most people, but he was content with his lot. Mencius praised them all, "Though Yu, Ji, and Yan Hui had different attitudes towards life, they are all benevolent people. Yu was concerned about the flood victims as if he himself had allowed them to drown; Ji was concerned about the famine victims as if he himself had allowed them to starve, and Yan Hui, had he been in the others' position, would have done the same."

CHAPTER V

Affairs of State

The sage and the ordinary person are all human beings.

During a talk on ancient sages, Gongsun Chou asked Mencius, "You are good at analyzing others' words and cultivating the great moral force. Since you are accomplished in both language and morality, you must be a sage. Are you?" Mencius replied, "When Zi Gong asked Confucius, 'Are you a sage?' Confucius said, 'I cannot be a sage. It is just that I never felt tired of learning and teaching.' Even Confucius didn't claim he was a sage, so how could you say I am a sage?" Mencius said. "Sages and ordinary people are all human beings. Their difference is that the former tend to stand out among the latter."

When a non-benevolent person holds a high post, he will extend his non-benevolence to the people.

Mencius said, "Even with the eyesight of Li Lou and the skill of Gongshu Ban, one cannot draw the perfect square and circle without the right tools. Even with the hearing of Shi Kuang, one cannot check the five notes without the help of six pitch pipes. Even with the capability of Yao and Shun, one cannot bring peace and prosperity into the empire without benevolence. Today some kings have benevolent intentions, but their people see no benefit. Their reigns therefore cannot last, for they fail to carry out the ways of the sages. Since the sages did their utmost to implement the rule of benevolence, benevolence is the universal morality. The platform should be built along a mountain; the pool should be dug in a marsh. Is it wise to run a state without following the ways of the ancient sages? For this reason, only the benevolent should be put in high positions. When a non-benevolent person holds a high post, he will extend his evil to the people, and chaos will result."

If a king regards his officials as his hands and feet, the officials will regard him as their hearts and bellies. If a king regards his officials as dogs and horses, the officials will regard him as a common citizen. If a king regards his officials as earth and trash, the officials will regard him as their enemy.

Mencius told King Xuan of Qi, "If a king regards his officials as his hands and feet, the officials will regard him as their hearts and bellies. If a king regards his officials as dogs and horses, the officials will regard him as a common citizen. If a king regards his officials as earth and trash, the officials will regard him as an enemy." The king asked, "According to the rites, former officials should mourn for the deceased king they have served. What should the king do to have his officials do so?" Mencius replied, "He should take their good advice, and therefore bring benefit to the people. When an official has to leave the state, the king should send people to escort him, and make arrangements beforehand in the place he is going to. The king will not take back the official's land and house unless the latter doesn't return in three years. By doing so, the king will be mourned by his former officials after death. Now, some kings won't hear the good advice of their officials. When an official has to leave the state for some reason, the king puts his family and relatives into prison, makes problems for him in the place he is going to, and confiscates his land and property immediately. This is the way to treat the enemy. How could one mourn his enemy?"

If one in a high position is keen on anything, his subordinates will be keener on it. A gentleman is like the wind, and a petty man is like the grass. The grass will always bend to the will of the wind.

After Duke Wen of Teng passed away, the Crown Prince sent his teacher, Ran You, to Mencius to consult with him regarding the funeral rites. Mencius said, "Though I have never studied the rites for kings, I have heard of them. The state should observe mourning for three years, as was stipulated in the Xia, Shang, and Zhou dynasties." The Crown Prince decided to take his advice, but encountered opposition from other members of the royal family and officials. He sent his teacher to Mencius for advice again. Mencius said, "It is the Crown Prince who should make the decision. If one in the high position is keen on anything, his subordinates will be keener on it. A gentleman is like wind, and a petty man is like grass. The grass will bend to the will of the wind." The Crown Prince eventually arranged the funeral for his father as Mencius suggested.

An official should resign if he cannot fulfill his duty; an advisor should resign if his advice is not taken.

Mencius told Chi Yuan of the state of Qi, "It is right for you to resign from the post of magistrate of Liqiu and take the post of judge so you can advise the king directly, but why haven't you given any advice to him since you took the office months ago?" Chi Yuan presented some advice to the king, but the king would not listen, so he resigned again. Some people then commented, "What Mencius told Chi Yuan is right, but will he do the same himself?" These words were brought to Mencius by his disciples. He said, "An official should resign if he cannot fulfill his duty; an advisor should resign if his advice is not taken. I am not in any official position, nor responsible for offering advice. So I have great freedom in deciding on whether I should stay or go."

The way to win a state is to win the support of its people; the way to win the support of the people is to win their hearts.

Mencius was learned, and was ready to answer others' questions. One day a man asked, "Emperor Jie of the Xia Dynasty and Emperor Zhou of the Shang Dynasty lost their reigns, why is this so?" Mencius said, "Because they were tyrannical and therefore lost the support of their people. The way to win a state is to win the support of its people; the way to win the support of the people is to win their hearts." The man further asked, "How did Emperor Tang of the Shang Dynasty and Emperor Wu of the Zhou Dynasty establish their rule?" Mencius said, "The people submit to benevolent and virtuous rulers. Tang and Wu implemented the rule of benevolence, and therefore won the support of their people. That's the reason why they held on to power. It is like how the water flows down to the lowland, and animals run towards the wild. It is like the otters that drive fish to deep ponds; it is like eagles that drive birds to forests. It is Jie and Zhou that drove the people towards Tang and Wu."

CHAPTER VI

Principles of Cultivation

A gentleman should not blame Heaven.

Mencius left the state of Qi for another place. On the way, his disciple Chong Yu thought his master looked unhappy, so he asked, "Sir, you do not seem to be happy. You once told me a gentleman should not blame Heaven or other people. Why can't you do that today?" Mencius answered, "The time has changed, and the situation is different. History shows that a sage ruler arises every 500 years, and someone famous for his talent and virtue will appear to assist him. It has been 700 years since the Zhou Dynasty was founded, and it is time to bring society back into order. If it is the Heaven's will to bring peace into the world, who can do the job except me? Why should I feel unhappy?"

A gentleman feels no shame when he raises his head toward Heaven or bows his head toward the people.

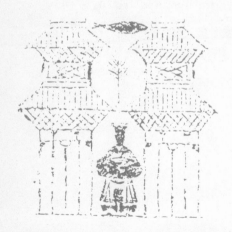

A disciple asked Mencius, "What are the delights of a gentleman?" Mencius replied, "A gentleman delights in three things, but being the king is not among them." The disciples asked, "What are they?" Mencius said, "The first delight is to have parents, the second delight is to feel no shame when one looks upward toward heaven or downward toward the faces of the people; the third delight is to gather talented people around the world and teach them. When a gentleman takes delight in these three things, he will give no thought to ruling the state."

The fact is that he will not do it, not that he is unable to do it.

King Xuan of Qi asked Mencius to tell him how Duke Huan of Qi and Duke Wen of Jin built their states into powerful kingdoms. Mencius said, "The disciples of Confucius never talked about them, so their stories have not been passed down. I have never heard of them either. But I would like to talk about the kingly way of unifying the world with morality." He further said, "If someone tells you, 'I can lift 3,000 catties, but cannot lift a feather; I can see fuzz on a bird, but cannot see a cartload of firewood.' Will you believe him?" The king answered, "Of course not." Mencius said, "If someone claims he cannot cross the North Sea carrying the Taishan Mountain under his arms, he means it. But if he claims he cannot break a branch for an elderly man, the fact is that he will not do it, not that he is unable to do it. Not following the kingly way is different from carrying the Taishan Mountain to cross the North Sea, but is the same as not breaking a branch for an elderly man. It is because you are unwilling to do it rather than are unable to do it."

Opportunity is more important than capability; the harvest is more important than the tilling.

Gongsun Chou visited Mencius, and talked about how the state is ruled. Gongsun Chou asked, "Do you think the state of Qi could unify the empire?" Mencius said, "Given the current situation, it is as easy as turning over one's hand for the state of Qi to do it." Gongsun Chou asked for more explanation, so Mencius said, "As a Qi saying goes, 'Opportunity is more important than capability; the farming season is more important than the hoeing.' The state of Qi has a vast territory and a huge population, and it will soon unify the empire if it implements the rule of benevolence." Seeing Gongsun Chou nodding in agreement, Mencius said, "This is the time when success is assured."

The most outstanding virtue of a gentleman is to do good things with others.

Mencius thought highly of Zi Lu, a disciple of Confucius. Mencius said, "Zi Lu was glad to have his errors pointed out, and Yu bowed down when he heard anything good. Shun was even more extraordinary. He kept learning from others, and took the jobs of farmer, potter, and fisherman before being appointed by the king. By learning good points from others, one can do good things together with them and therefore do good things to others. The most outstanding virtue of a gentleman is to do good things together with others."

Everyone has sympathy.

齊桓公

King Xuan of Qi asked Mencius how Duke Huan of Qi and Duke Wen of Jin built their states into powers, hinting that he wanted to accomplish the same, but Mencius urged him to practice the kingly way. The king, therefore, had to ask, "What virtues are required to unify the world?" Mencius answered, "If you intend to unify the world out of the purpose of bringing your people a peaceful life, no one can stop you." The king asked, "Can someone like me do it?" "Yes," Mencius said. "I was told Your Highness didn't even have the heart to slaughter an ox as sacrifice to the bell. I understand that it is because you feel sympathy. One with the heart of mercy will be able to unify the world."

Human nature is good. Water always flows downward.

Gao Zi asserted, "Human nature is like running water, It runs to the east if there is a breach in the east, and it runs to the west if there is a breach in the west. Human nature is not inherently good nor evil, just like water, it may run toward the east or west." Mencius retorted, "Though water may run towards the east or west, isn't it a rule for water to run from the high to the low? Human nature is good, just like water always flows downward. Of course, when disturbed, water can shoot high up above one's forehead; when driven by instruments, it can flow upward against laws of nature. But can these be attributed to the nature of water? No, it is because of external forces. One can do evil, because one's nature can be changed just as the flow of water can be changed by external forces."

One who practices justice and benevolence will be helped and supported by many; one who doesn't practice justice and benevolence will be helped and supported by few.

Mencius said, "Favorable weather is less important than advantageous geographical position, and advantageous geographical position is less important than the unity of people. For instance, a small city is only three square *li* in its inner city and seven square li in its outer city, and cannot be seized by the enemy army after a long siege. During this period, there must be weather favorable to the besiegers, but they cannot break into the city, because an advantageous geographical position is more important than favorable weather. Despite its high city wall, deep moat, fine weapons and abundant reserves of supplies, its defenders abandoned it and fled the moment the enemies arrived. This is because unity of people is more important than an advantageous geographical position. Boundaries alone cannot stop people from fleeing, precipitous terrain alone cannot insure national security, and force alone cannot subjugate the world. One who practices justice and benevolence will be helped and supported by many people; one who does not practice justice and benevolence will be helped and supported by few. If one is detested by the people, even his relatives will turn against him; if one is supported by the people, all in the world will submit to him."

When Confucius ascended East Mountain, he realized how small the state of Lu was; when he ascended Taishan Mountain, he realized how small the empire was.

Mencius told his disciples, "When Confucius ascended the East Mountain, he realized how small the state of Lu was; when he ascended Taishan Mountain, he realized how small the empire was. Therefore, one cannot talk about rivers with those who have seen the sea; and one cannot talk about doctrines of other schools of thought with those who live with sages. The way to view water is to admire its magnificent waves. The bright light of sun and moon can reach every corner, even the smallest crevice. Water will not pursue its journey until it has filled all of the lowlands. Gentlemen who are determined to study grand principles cannot reach enlightenment without making some achievement first."

A courteous person will not insult; a frugal person will not pillage.

One day Mencius overheard his disciples talking about their understanding of courtesy and frugality. Some said a courteous person is amicable and knows what to say and what not to. Others contended that a frugal person uses things prudently. They argued hotly, and could not convince each other, so they went to Mencius for help. Mencius said, "A courteous person will not insult others; a frugal person will not pillage others. How can one be really courteous or frugal if he insults or robs others to make them submissive, though he claims he is? Are the virtues of courtesy and frugality merely nice words and big smiles?"

One learns the weight after weighing it; one learns the length after measuring it. This principle can be applied to everything.

One day King Xuan of Qi saw a man leading a cow past the palace, and asked, "Where are you taking it?" "To the sacrifice," came the reply. The king felt sympathy for the trembling animal, so he ordered that it be spared. Mencius took this opportunity to persuade the king to practice benevolent policies. He asked, "Why can Your Highness bestow favor on animals but not on your people? One finds out the weight after weighing it; one finds out the length after measuring it. This principle can be applied to everything."

When one conquers by way of force, the people won't submit willingly. When one conquers by virtue and morality, the people will follow.

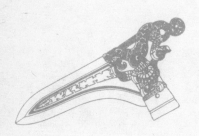

One day someone asked Mencius, "Since one can dominate the world both by way of force and morality, isn't it reasonable that the rule of force and the rule of benevolence coexist?" Mencius replied, "It is true that one state can dominate the world by using force, but it can only be achieved after it grows big, powerful, and rich. To dominate by virtue of morality is different. The rule of benevolence can win wide support, and consequently make the state bigger and stronger. That explains why Emperor Tang of the Shang Dynasty and Emperor Wen of the Zhou Dynasty started with small territories of 70 and 100 square *li* respectively, but both built their states into great powers." The man nodded. Mencius further said, "When one conquers others by way of force, they don't submit to him willingly, but they will when one conquers them by virtue of morality."

The soldier who retreats 50 paces mocks the one who retreats 100.

After a long and hard journey, Mencius and his disciples arrived in the Daliang, capital of the state of Wei. But there the King of Wei gave them the cold shoulder. He didn't greet them when they arrives, nor did he arrange a welcoming banquet, nor even come to consult with Mencius on politics. The next day, Mencius was introduced to the King. The moment he saw Mencius, the King asked abruptly, "You come to my state from a thousand *li* away, don't you bring us any benefit?" During their second meeting, Mencius persuaded the King to share his enjoyment with the people, arousing his interest in rule of benevolence. So when they met a third time, the King asked, "I have done my utmost to run the state. After inspecting the neighboring states, I find that none of their kings is as concerned about the people as I am. Why don't they come to my land to seek refuge?" Mencius said, "In combat, armies of the two sides clash. Some soldiers drop their armor and weapons and flee. One who retreats 50 paces mocks the one who retreats 100 for cowardice. Is he right?" "No," replied the King, "Because he also flees. The only difference is that he doesn't run as far as the other." Mencius nodded, "As Your Highness can understand this, you should not expect people of the neighboring states to seek refuge with you."

Notes to Illustrations

Cover. Ancient style of the Chinese character "Meng" (from which the word Mencius originates).

p3. Portrait of Mencius.

p4. A wood-block image of Menius in ancient China.

p7. Bronze statue of General Huo Qubing in Five Spring Park, Lanzhou, Gansu Province.

p13. King Wengong (cong'er) of the Jin Dynasty (265-420), a wood-block image in ancient China.

p17. Home of Mencius, Shandong Province.

p19. A wood-block image depicting vase-making in ancient China.

p22. Song Dynasty (960-1279) edition of *Mencius* by wood-block printing.

p25. Statue of Mencius.

p29. Portrait of Emperor Li Shimin of the Tang Dynasty (618-907).

p33. A wood-block image of farming in ancient China.

p35. A wood-block image of King Xuan of the Zhou Dynasty (1100-221 BC).

p42. A wood-block image of King Ping of the Zhou Dynasty.

p43. Archway of the hometown of Mencius in Shandong.

p46. *Notes to Mencius* by wood-block printing, written by Dai Zhen of Qing Dynasty (1644-1911).

p49. Sculpture of Mencius' mother teaching her son.

p58. A wood-block image of teaching in ancient China.

p60. Portrait of King Yu of the Xia Dynasty (2100-1600 BC).

p63. "Ramping on the Huns." Sculpture attributed to the time of General Huo Qubing of the Han Dynasty (206 BC-AD 220).

p68. *Picking Roses* by Li Tang of the Song Dyansty (960-1279). This painting tells the story of Bo Yi and Shu Qi of the Shang Dynasty (1600-1100 BC), who refused to receive pay from the Zhou empire (1100-211 BC) and instead picked roses to eat as food until death.

p71. Stone tablets in the Temple of Mencius in Shandong.

p72. A wood-block image of Guan Zhong, a famous politician during the Spring and Autumn Period (770-476 BC).

p91. *Providing Relief*, a wood-block painting in ancient China.

p92. A soldier of the terracotta army of the First Emperor of the Qin Dynasty (221-207 BC).

p95. A wood-block image of Mencius in ancient China.

p96. A wood-block image of Xu Mian, a high official of the Tang Dynasty (618-907).

p98. Porcelain figures of the rat, ox, and monkey, unearthed from Guizi Mountain at Wuchang, Hubei Province, 1955.

p102. A stone-carving from the Han Dynasty, unearthed from Jiaxiang, Shandong Province.

p103. Portrait of Mencius.

p110. Part of the painting by Zhou Wenju of the Five Dynasties (907-960) about a gathering of poets.

p113. Portrait of Mencius.

p114. Statue of Mencius, a gift to a Japanese university from the Information Office